his book is dedicated to

-    abuse survivors
-    the parentified child
- those who have gone no contact with a parent
- and every wandering soul who has lived with mental illness.

You are so much more than your pain

I love you so

I was alone
resigned to a life of wading through uncharted waters, my life.

I didn't choose death.

I chose to take an ax to my life instead. I set it all aflame and watched it all burn; comforting embers. I tore it to shreds. You will never touch me again.

I left.

Who am I now?

What does it all mean?

Where do I go after letting go
of that sinking ship full of everything I know?

My memories are detached from the bounds of reality.
They have created a force of their own; desolate
static cradling the ruins of my psyche. They don't
fully belong to me.

In order to reclaim my life, I must sift through the
fragmented pieces of myself.

The last thing I thought I would do was pick up a pen,
but after all this time

my inner child deserves to have someone bear witness
to it all.

"Through the Looking Glass"

ISBN [979-8-218-26085-9] (Paperback)

Library of Congress Control Number: 2023914170

This is a work of creative nonfiction. Any resemblance to actual persons, living or dead, events, or locales is entirely coincidental. The events and conversations in this book have been set down to the best of the author's ability, although some names and details have been changed to protect the privacy of individuals. Some parts have been fictionalized in varying degrees, for various purposes. Names, characters, places, and incidents either are the product of the author's imagination or are used fictitiously

Book Cover by Elodie Rose

First Edition: 2023

I don't want to be an adult.

I want cascading fireflies

and clear night skies.

I want techno beats with a side of glitter
doused in cheap liquor.

I dream of adrenaline rushes and problems as deep as reality
TV.

I want movie moments

A montage of perfectly crafted heartwarming scenes set to a
laugh track.

The wonders of teenage hope and anguish endlessly racing
across my screen.

But I don't see them in *my* memories.

"Untitled"

mother,
You did not prepare me for how hard this life would be.

But I am not here to talk about my mother.

I am here to talk about Mama.

A term of endearment
my mother did not earn.

Mama, is the woman with warm busty bosoms,
emotional intelligence through the roof telling you
it's going to be alright.

Mama, teaches you how to protect yourself against this world. Against
men foaming at the mouth to take your tenderness right from under
you.

Mama?

A Mama is supposed to learn and teach

Guide, be gentle, and don't preach.

Don't overbear, don't leach.

Dichotomy is your middle name when you're a Mama

Oh mother, how I have always wanted a Mama.

But you didn't even know how to be a woman, mother

So how could you be a Mama?

You were just a little girl hell-bent on burning others to keep yourself warm.

mother I am better than you now,

Did you know that?

I reclaimed myself from the misery of your aftermath.

And yet I hear you're still out there in the distance
Burning others to keep yourself warm.

I do not know how you *still* do it.

mother, you would not believe this,
others call me Mama now.

No, they are not the fruit of my womb

They are the saltine tears, and long-lasting love and commitment through these weary years.

I Learn

I Teach.

I Guide.

I'm gentle

And I don't Preach.

I don't Overbear

Don't Leach.

Dichotomy is my middle name

Oh mother, I am a Mama.

M a m a

Silence serenades us
For this is our moment.
I'm sorry it took so long for me to sit beside you.

As I sit here, I beg you to lay down your burdens.
I forgive you.

I still hear the softness of your voice
The depth of your love.
You made every breath sweeter
And every waking day brighter.

It echoes, the day I lost you
so near to my soul.

It was days, weeks, months, maybe decades ago.
Time means everything
and nothing since you have been gone.
I don't want to make new memories without you.

I wanted to sit beside you.
I wanted to sit at your side for everything.
I would have walked through the valley of death at your side.
But now, I am stuck on the other side.
Fated to walk this life without you by my side.

I chose denial.
I withdrew.
I am lost.
I still look for you.

The loss of you will be my undoing.

We guided each other.
Collaborated in everything we do.

No greater nurturer than I.
Not a more gracious watchdog than you.
Who am I without you at my side?

The infinite stars and constellations do not need you.
They do not deserve you.

I sit beside you as my soul crumbles into this earth
 just so I can lay beside you
 One last time.

I am fragile, I am frail.
I feel myself withering away.
I am holding on to a fleeting sense of sanity

So selfishly,
I finally came to see you.

I need you to tell me that you're okay.
In the silence, and the warmth of the wind's embrace
I hear sweet music.
The kind we used to listen to.
I feel contentment, peace, and rest.
Maybe I just want it to be true.

All I know is that
I love you.

So I sit,
weeping
beside you.

"Only the good die young"

Amidst scintillating stories of my own helplessness, you told me only you could guide me to the promised land.

Only you could determine my worth.

We could only survive this life strapped to each other's side like armor. I believed you.

So, I followed you…

I don't know when the tide turned
but one day I found myself
Feigning the loyalty and affection I had once given you so freely.

I no longer *wanted* to gain your approval.

I no longer believed you could grant me **"worth"**
because I was having trouble seeing any in *you*.

Codependency

8 fun facts my mental illnesses do not want you to know.

A letter to my brother

1. Did you know that when you talk to me we always have company? Mental illness settles in, distorting all of my memories. She accompanies me to everything. She doesn't even ask if she's allowed to come. She has claimed my body and my mind as her own.

2. Did you know anxiety is my jailer? She imprisoned me in my own inner world. Clever and cunning. Cutting me off from the world. She said it's to spare me. *"Hurt and humiliation is the only thing that waits for you outside these bars."* My anxiety is brilliant in that way. She keeps me on my toes. Incapacitated from the constant emotional whiplash. My anxiety reminds me, there can be hell on earth.

3. Did you know that Depression suffocates me so sweetly I forget she is an enemy at all? She strokes my hair and we make pacts I pinky swear to keep. She makes my weary heart soar with promises of peace. Her lips taste like whiskey. I like the way it burns. She whispers to me about a world where I am no longer in it. The smell of her lingers in my bed.

4. Did you know I feel guilty every time you've had to nurture me? To care for me as the last of my light faded away. You held my hand through uncharted waters. You kept me afloat with loving hands and worried eyes. I hate the pain you've had to endure to stand beside me. And I don't know how to make it better.

5. Did you know that I worry I may lack the ability to truly be happy? Can a person with a past like mine ever even come close to happiness or contentment? Will I always be haunted by the horrors of my past and the magnitude of my failures? Did you know these questions keep me up at night?

6. Did you know that being depressed can feel like waves of agony washing over you, *Over and Over*, while your lungs constrict? You can not breathe. You can not cope. Your eyes blur and your body trembles. You try to remember the last time you were even in charge of your own body.

7. Did you know that I feel helpless? Over time it has turned to shame. And Shame will waste no time making itself home in your head. He's rancid, persistent, impervious to logic, and has an intimate understanding of my flaws. I am desperate to find relief.

8. Did you know that when my perception of the world is narrowed and my fears take hold, memories of you can always bring me to shore?

I write poetry to comfort myself.

A poem, like lyrics
take on a life of its own every time
someone hears it.

Every time someone reads it.

Every time someone speaks it.

Every time someone needs it.

Life.

Perhaps, I just like creating life.

Feeding the ferocity of my Femininity.

Creating everything and....

Anything

So I never have to sit with nothing.

"I am no poet."

Prayer,

the desperate man's last cry for salvation.

In the midnight sky, there is beauty
in the depth of her darkness.

I ask the starlights,

"What is it like beyond the sky?"

I am a desperate woman:

not only seeking salvation

I long for revelation.

In the shattered pieces of me: there are no epiphanies.

I do not seek riches or redemption.

I fall before you praying for mercy.

I still see the rituals of indoctrination

Crimson wine, Communion wafers, and the so-called Gospel of the Lord.

I lost faith a long time ago, in the hallowed halls of gorgeous cathedrals.

Now, I can only feel the majesty of the Universe when I look at the stars.

I can feel the earth beneath my feet. I can reach out towards that unrelenting sky.

It is here that I feel holy.

I know man's limited brain cannot begin to capture all that you are.

Great Forces that be,

I stand before you, naked

Praying for mercy.

Please Deliver me

to a better tomorrow.

Movie nights with you always feel shiny and new,
like unboxing Christmas presents at the birth of sunrise.

There is a vibrancy in your eyes
as I show you all the little things I love.

The glimmer of old movies on the tv screen.

soda

popcorn breath

and candy-stained sheets.

Doe eyes, adolescent giggles, hands stealing sweet touches
underneath blankets.

A blooming love under the Iridescent Embers of string lights.

Healing in the impromptu dance sessions.

Healing in your arms.

Healing in your touch.

"I love you" escapes my lips

 and enters the soundtrack of our picture-perfect love.

We craft whole worlds with inside jokes with these old movies as our catalyst

Everything about this night is sweet.
Planning midnight rendezvous like kids who have finally dared to dream.

So suddenly,

And without warning

The laws of time remind us
we have to sleep.

We whisper sweet nothings to each other
until we can reach our dreams.

"Movie Nights"

Sometimes, death feels safer than life.

Will I ever be free?

I have abandoned the notion that blood
keeps you imprisoned to venomous people.

My life is less burdensome without you in it.

You....

kept me bound in the darkness for so long

I forgot about the Sun's warmth.

I feel like I am alive for the very first time.

In the thrill of it all.....

                        I forgot this was supposed to be a loss.

**When I think
of my departure from you and
everything you are**

I only mourn
what you should have been.
I do not miss you.

No-Contact

I am sick of swiping through meaningless apps
devoid of true connection
and full of meaningless sex.

I want a great love, not a fleeting lust,
that will dissipate upon the rise of the morning sun.
I want a love that carves its way into the history books.

I want someone to tell me that I am so effervescent
I must have been kissed by the stars.
Hand selected by God herself to walk among the earth
and illuminate the world with my beauty.

I want to know what it feels like to be in love.
A love that frightens and challenges me.

I want to be your medicine
your guide
and your confidant.

       And yes, I want to be your lover

I want to know your body better than my own.
I want to touch you forever.
In love with the certainty that nothing about our love is fleeting.
I want to hold you when you feel like you are on the precipice of
defeat.

I want to know your story.
I want to explore the catacombs of your pain...
I want you to know
that I see you
and still I
choose you.

I want to assure you every day, that you are a force not of this world
dear. So never stoop to any mere ordinary human's level.

Even if that means walking away.

Even if it means Change,
Compromises,
Sacrifice.

Be my advocate and biggest supporter and I shall be yours.

One day I will meet you my love,

perhaps through a sea of meaningless swipes

"Dating Apps"

You were in pursuit of a
perfect puppet
to give you purpose

And that is how you first met me.

I was everything.
Precious, untainted by the harshest truths of this world.

It's so predictable now-
how this story ends

A mother in pursuit of a poised and righteous daughter
Shatters her into pieces.

I perched you on a pedestal and prayed for a miracle.
What is the price of your approval?
Will it be enough to earn my peace?

My successes paled in comparison
to the failures you were trying to avenge through me.

I was not permitted to be my own person.

Feelings equated to Weakness

Weakness = pathetic

I prayed at the altar of your expectations,

I received nothing but scorn. I would have even taken pity.

Something

Anything
That resembled sympathy.
I was decorative, only to be seen when useful to your pristine image.

A tale of handcrafted curated perfection,
created to soothe an ailing marriage
impress your relatives
and appease your crippling insecurities.

Everything was

        about you.

No wonder I went bat-shit crazy
My mind fragmented under the weight of needing
to be perfect, *knowing* it would never quite be enough.

You broke me
down.

and it took me a long fucking time to get back up.

I had to learn to walk free
of the strings, you used to keep me in bondage.

And then-

Time gifted me perspective.

Pray tell,

Did you like the fleeting power it gave you- to assert your dominance
over a child?

-I am not your fucking puppet.

When people are afraid, I take notice.

The camaraderie of fear has formed, unified, and sanctified communities.

Humans do insane shit once fear has taken hold, a clever hand can turn a tide into hysteria.

Fear is humanity's greatest catalyst.

Fear is a tool.

Who do you love?

because the prospect of loss will bring fear bubbling up to the surface.

What are you willing to do to protect the ones you love; the things you value?

When you know how to wield it - psychological torment can be as effective as the edge of Micheal's sword.

Fear lays all our cards on the table at once. An open heart.

What will you do with it?

Before you answer that, heed this warning

*"there is **nothing** more dangerous than a man with nothing left to lose."*

\-   *Viva la Vida*

If I was the eye of your affection how would you behold me?

"Mona"

Dissociation

I feel nothing
except the silent waves of sadness crashing over me.
Floating
In this deafening void.

I don't know.

I used to write long romantic poems
Filled with passion and agony.
I used to write about picking up the pieces
of all that has been broken.

And now there are no pieces.
No beautifully shattered mosaic
at the center of my heart.

I don't *want* to know.
I just wanna die.

My hands tremble when I realize there is nothing left.
There are no more pieces to grasp onto, they have been reduced to ashes.
The pieces of my heart have shattered into dust.

There is a lump in my throat and fog in my mind
Thinking of my youth where I had it all figured out.
And when I didn't
I would scour the earth to find it.

There was no one more fearless.

now when i wake i know
I *have* to live.
Not out of youth, passion, or desire
But out of obligation.

And I am scared because I am no longer afraid to die.
I am afraid to live.

In the moments I can't bear it anymore
I find myself floating in the boundless void.

It feels as if you're suspended in radio static.

It knows no time.
It knows no judgments.
It has no expectations, pressures or deadlines.
It holds no pain, resentment or fear.
It is my void.
It is nothingness

When I exit my void.
I enter the world dazed.

What's wrong?
People will say.

And I say
 I don't know.

People will say
You have a great life.
And I say
"I know."

The problem is I can't fucking feel it.

The only thing I feel is this deep, profound sadness
And with every single breath, it tells me to lay down my weapons.

I no longer have the will to fight.

so I go walk on the sand.
I hear the wind howling.
Mother Earth is calling me.
To return to the earth.

And then, all I hear is radio static.

*How lovely would it be to sink my teeth into your flesh, I think
as the room is consumed by carnivorous Gasping Breaths.*

Your scent is sweet
like rose water and lilacs.

It reminds me to take my time with you.

You need loving, worship.
I must devour you to show my adoration.

I take off all the Barriers between us.

kissing up and down your legs.

You grant me an open invitation.

I wait, despite my thirst.

I tease, despite my hunger.

You start making waves with your hips inviting me to take a swim.

my breath feels like a warning in my chest.

I am about to give in.

I go up to your face to kiss you
And Now You Are Ferocious.

Sweet retribution.
You want me bare.

Who am I not to give it to you?

I smile between deep kisses and all sorts of sensations.
Until the throbbing in my ears
    and other regions halt.

        there's a knock on the door....

        Room Service

I WILL NOT STOOP TO GRASP WHAT I AM OWED.

I WILL LET KARMA COLLECT ON YOUR DEBT.

I WILL NO LONGER DIM MY LIGHT TO ATTEND TO YOU.

REVENGE

Surreptitiously, you gained access to my heart.

I didn't know you were there to break it - in ways, I still cannot fathom.

You ingratiated yourself into my life and my family.
I thought you were kind and harmless.

I soon learned
the cost of being wrong.

To this day, my breath still gets caught in the back of my throat when I make decisions.

You slithered into my life to teach me the crippling anguish of betrayal.

Innocently, I thought you were someone who resided at the intersection of family and friend.
Before, you gave yourself access to my body without permission.

Mischievous, Sly, Brutal and Cunning.

This was a game of Cat and mouse to you.

Predator and prey

Perpetrator and victim.

That is when I was really scared..

This was a game to you.

Everything I threw you caught; your face lit up with amusement. You liked the fight and the pain you were inflicting.

Betrayal   *Betrayal*

Violence and Terror.

Forced Entry

                    Disgust   *Disgust*

          Disgust   *Disgust*

                    I was a child.

Disgust   *Digust*   *Digustl*

Who were you?

Fear Fear Fear

What other snakes were looming in the midst disguising themselves as friends?

Fear   *Fear*   *Fear*

Why didn't I see this coming?

Shame   *Shame*   *Shame*

                              Betrayal

            Betrayal

                    Betrayal

"Fʊᴄᴋ ʏᴏᴜ!" I hiss

I claw, writhe and scrape

   I scream and kick.

Terror seeps into my core.

I'm afraid I will never go home.

Stop!

No!

Let me go!

PLEASE

Heart
breaks.

I manage to escape.

My body aches.

And I
will never be the same.

"Trust Issues"

Storytelling (in all her forms) is humanity's most redeeming quality. Stories gift us the opportunity to be a part of something greater than ourselves.

I love when I get the chance to listen.

When someone tells you a story they invite you to be a part of something they have created. Something they have lived through, or a masterful blend of both.

Our lived experiences make us human.
The lessons and insights we earn from our unique perspectives can help us connect with others.

I have always found this practice quite beautiful.

When I was little I coveted books.
I fell in love with the authors that gifted us their raw soul and flesh sprawled out on the page
for us to read.

I would spend hours escaping into new lives.

Whimsical adventures, delighted by the giggles I stifled,
as laughter lifted from the page and stuffed itself into my cheeks.
Exploring the catacombs of each character's psyche
Wide-eyed as I absorbed the magic.

Books were my first best friend.

Poems were my heart.

Poems are the most honest declaration of the human spirit.
Unfiltered | raw and authentic testimony.

They challenge you to reflect.

Later on, musicals encapsulated my vibrant queer spirit
The sheer vibrancy of the theater
The dedication, excellence, and theatricality it took.

I wrote stories for the stage to bring to life. All the cascading elements,
and people coming together to make the story come to life.

I recall my own life as a series of short stories that one day I will have
the courage to tell.

"Untitled"

I rang in my 21st birthday alone with a mocktail in my hand.

The people I live with, I don't much care for anymore. Who wants to celebrate with cowards, liars who deceive and abandon you?

I hear the sting of their betrayal in their silence, as the clock strikes midnight.

My real family are safely tucked away snoring on my screen.

I have never felt more lonely.

"Happy Birthday to Me."

Public Service Announcement

I promise you: I no longer extend energy to
you - in any capacity.

I revoked your access to me.

The problem was, somehow you came to
believe that access to me was a right.

Not a privilege I can ignite and extinguish
whenever I damn well please.

Simply put, I will no longer beg to be seen
as worthy and I won't beg for common
decency.

I am a human and I reserve the right to be
treated that way.

I have removed you from my life and
continue to elevate higher.

I got therapy bills and a fresh new
attitude.

I am learning. I am growing. I am
processing. I am recovering.
I am healing.

I am moving the hell on.

Your "love" no longer fits in with who I am
and this new life I have fought to build. I
revoked your access to me to protect
myself.

So if you seek my destruction now, instead
of looking within yourself,

You disgust me.
I pity you. And most of all, I bid you
farewell.

No-Contact *(the Sequel)*

Interlude I

"It's not fair to deny me of the cross I bear, that you gave to me"

You Oughta Know

by Alanis Morissette

As I cried my heart out, I screamed those words into my pillow. Every night I was a puddle of anguish and confusion until finally I was handed four little letters.

I was handed those four letters so formally. I can still hear the crisp rip of the prescription pad. The sting of the cold AC. The ugly yellow linoleum beneath my feet.

PTSD. I was politely informed that my case fell under the purview of Complex PTSD. It was treatable, slightly different from PTSD, and hadn't made her debut into the DSM-5 yet.

It's actually one of my happier college memories.

I thought I was going bat-shit crazy. I mopped the hallways to my lecture halls with my tears. I was too scared to be in public anymore. I was riddled with fear. Anxiety took away my breath and made every moment feel insurmountable. Everything got out of hand, and I found myself bedridden.

So, there I was, sitting in that cramped little office getting a diagnosis that meant the world to me.

I stumbled out of the office into the streets.

I was disoriented but still found a way to walk the side streets back home.

No one seemed to notice...

It was raining lightly.

The pitter patter of the rain was cleansing along my skin.

I felt a new era being ushered in.

After years of being gaslit. I had medical professionals assuring me that the abuse was real, and that it had very real consequences.

I was walking along watching the cars and buses zip on by. I got a cruel and brutal joke in the form of a phone call.

All I can think of are the words I once wailed into my pillow. It's not fair to deny ME of the cross I bear that YOU gave to me.

I think I knew in that moment
It was over.

How *dare you* deny me the cross I bear, that you gave to me?

I was a product of love.

Hm..

I should say

I was a product of the *pursuit* of love.

There is a difference,
A subtle one at that,
but a difference nonetheless.

My father wanted to love my mother.
My mother was too insecure.

She needed a new life, to revitalize her marriage.

A daughter to mold into the vision of herself that never came to be.

A ragdoll she could dress up all pretty and leave when she was bored.

A trophy to display to all of her "friends."

A thing she could beat into submission.

I hated her.

The favor was returned once she realized a darling little girl would not keep the father around.

Contempt and confusion were the themes of my childhood.

The weight of her disappointments sunk on her face, befallen and sad

She saw them in her daughter

"Rejection"

You.

You cut out my tongue. And then you spoke of an exalted future full of prestige and fortune- the one I had to build. You beat me into submission in order to mold me in your image. This child will be the mirror through which you transcend time to live as a young woman once more. This golden child will bring back riches

I.

I soothed your untamed ailments under the threat of death. I tended to your every whim. The years weighed heavy on my face and my face began to resemble yours. After all, I am made in your image. I bore the crushing weight of our failures and none of the acclaim from "our" accomplishments. You made a mockery of my tears. In your orbit, I lost myself.

Spiders in a Jar

Abstract
Eclectic and all things wonderful.

I clutch the necklace that you gave me.

There's a comfort in it.

The gold necklace of Queen Nefertiti rests on a golden pendant on my chest

Femininity exudes from it.

I felt connected to it the minute I put it on.

It felt like something I had wanted for a very long time.

A touchstone to home.

A gift that was valuable and thoughtful.

A motherless daughter meets

The most wonderful and eclectic person they have ever met,

who just so happens to be a childless mother

Serendipity.

When I touch this necklace

I am reminded that I did receive the authentic motherly love, I
never thought I would earn

I have it in the most unconventional way-
From the most eclectic and wonderful woman I will ever know.

21st Birthday Gift

I sealed our suicide note with a kiss.

Love was the final nail in my coffin.

My heart steadied
but my hands were still sweaty

I really meant it
when I said I would sacrifice myself for you.

Is that devotion, the stuff of fairytale books
Or obsession?

I would lay down my life for you.

You have me wrapped up tightly in the grips of our madness and all I
can see is you.

Milk and Honey dripping from your lips.

I knew I would not come out of this unscathed from the moment we
met.

I succumbed to the thrill of you.

Your breath on mine begging for the air to become one; for us to
become one.

We are not picture-perfect.

But
Together we create perfect moments -
we are constellations, stars fated for a greater purpose.

The moment our eyes meet with the intensity of the night sky;
Captivating

Meant to be.

Inexplicably, lulled by your Gravitational pull.

We are broken people who immortalized a love that was never fit to last.

Our love was great.

We are fossilized

Things like us can only last for a limited time.

Storybook love is tragic, fleeting

The kind of stuff that pulls at the heartstrings-

Enticing people to tell our story over and over and over again.

Until my darling we become history.
Pages in storybooks mulled over by English teachers.

The madness of temptation.

Two birds drunk on delusion
flying way too close to the sun.

R & J

The timer on the counter is set for 5 minutes.

There were streaks of paint across the woman's body,
Vibrant hues marking her shame

She enters the shower.
So the ritual can begin.

The Catharsis of Cleansing the body.
Rejoicing in the water's embrace.

She thinks of her lover as the streaks of paint refuse to fall off her body.

It is of no use. Her heart will not release her from the bonds of guilt. As she writhed in the throes of shame, her sanity slipped away. Peace and its virtues were lost to the girl now. Replaced by remorse. Overwhelmed by the sum of her choices. She indulged in a sinful union. She recalls the pleasure of longing. Forbidden fruit. She washes her hair with lilac-scented shampoo, hoping to rid herself of the speckled paint that now adorns her hair. Her lover was giving, so he marked her as his own. Unveiled the heat of her passion. Worshiped at the altar of her flesh. She granted him divine entry. She knew that the sins of night will always be revealed by the light, it's only a matter of time.

The clock struck 5, the alarm blasted through the air. She turned off the water. No test was needed to tell her what she already knew. The sacrament of lust has laid onto the world, a new life.

"REGRET"

Looking back, I see us as the kids we were.

They describe adolescents defining characteristics
As entitled,

prone to thinking they know everything.

While that might be true for some
It wasn't true for us.

We gathered knowledge like cannon fodder
desperate to protect ourselves with it.

In a world of ever-changing uncertainties, we exchanged knowledge
like currency.

It was essential to know what and who had been claimed.
It was essential to have allies to tell you where you should not be and
when.

We languished in fear and clung to each other
In the grass, pondering our place in the bigger picture and trying to
figure out what part we play.

I watched you disillusioned

and wished I had an image to lose.

I never had any childhood fallacies of hope to lose.

There was no fantasy that was crafted by misguided and
well-meaning adults.

I watched you grow wide-eyed into the sea of lies and meet me
where I had always been

Fucking Terrified, grappling with the horrors of this twisted reality.

If I had lied to myself, I would not have survived

I see that now, but that doesn't make it right.

You saw right through me, you were good at that

Far before I told you, you knew.

You didn't call me strong,

you gave me permission to cry.

You told me it was fucked up

and you were right.

And we were just kids.

To the boy, I thought I could love

To the people I have survived,

Don't you dare apologize to me. The apology will not fall upon deaf ears. If you truly have changed, I want you to go forth and use that energy with the people who are in your life now. No words you could muster up the courage to say to me would change that our relationship has ceased. It's far too little, far too late. It's done.

Go forth and be better for those who *are* in your life.

Apologize to **them**. I honored and validated my experience, my body, my hurt, and my peace when I walked away. I do not need you to do that for me. Your words are of no service to me. I will not absolve you of any guilt you may feel - that is your cross to bear.

I don't want an apology. To you, I am just a memory and perhaps - mercifully, a lesson learned. That is the best thing that can come out of all of my pain, that you *learn* not to harm people. And if that happens; it's entirely up to you.

If you are apologizing as some sort of last-ditch effort to get me to re-enter your life - seek therapy. Your delusion is now a cause for concern. Our relationship is over.

To all the people I have survived, there is absolutely nothing of value you can give to me.

I honor myself and my experience, my body, my hurt, and my peace by leading this life without you.

Do not contact me.

Go forth and do better.

To the people,

I have survived.

Benevolent

Kind

Intuitive

Wise.

Transcendent and Angelic.

Feminine and Iridescent.

Ethereal and Warm.

She connects to the earth
in all her majesty

Theatrical and Gracious

Eclectic and Authentic

Fruitful and Unrelenting

CREATION AND DESTRUCTION

The strength deep in her bones resonates
it cannot be contained
A celestial force that masks all fear.

It makes it so

She is Able
to fortify
and nurture young minds.

So she can be

A Pillar of hope,
A Lighthouse in every storm,
Considerate and Accommodating.

THAT IS THE KIND OF WOMAN I AM.

The woman I fight to be every day.

I think about my womanhood and femininity very deeply.
This intangible spiritual and sacred entity I have the privilege to possess

I think deeply about my sisters.
The kind of woman I am involves the content of my innermost being,
not my genitalia.

Being a woman looks and feels different for everyone.

I love *all* of my sisters so dearly.

The backgrounds we come from and the paths we walk are varied and
difficult.
I think these differences ought to be exalted.
Alas, it seems we too succumb to the most derivative human instinct
we have,
fanning the flames of acrimony and division among our own.

A measure of a woman is her willingness to walk alongside her sisters
unburdened by the surreptitious snake of competition.

The ability to uplift, support and facilitate the advancement of her
sisters.

To heal any and all inner misogyny that ails her so she can see that
another's spotlight does not deter or diminish her own

To unlearn and dismantle *all* the barriers that prevent us from seeing and respecting one another.

White supremacy, racism, transphobia, xenophobia, homophobia

All of it.

I know that this is not accessible to every woman and some would not even be willing to engage in such self-reflection.

The truth is

The more clarity I gain for myself,
 the more I want it for everyone else.

FEMME

For as long as my light exists I will love you.
In this world and the next.

The essence of my being loves you.
I know this to be true as I know the sky is blue

Our love is a profound entity – almost sacred in nature

I believe it can last through many lifetimes, transcending time and space

In fact, I believe they have already gone on all sorts of adventures far beyond our comprehension.

I pray there will be many more.

I am not a religious woman, but somehow I have faith in us.

My love for you is the most honest thing about me.

Everlasting and Persistent

There is nothing more pure than my love for you.

No matter the battle I will fight at your side.

Until the end of our time.

I will choose you.

- *E*

A new life has come into fruition
and a funeral is in order.

I must say goodbye to that girl before me
she knew how to survive.
and she sure as hell never got her flowers.

I honor her now.

Metamorphosis was a hard-fought battle.

I am grateful for the flowers I adorned in my hair, white orchids

I lie my past self to rest with all the pomp and circumstance she's
owed

I feel love swelling in my heart for her now, gratitude and sorrow

The other patrons don't recognize me.
I pay them no mind as I lay a single kiss on your forehead,
appreciation and reverence for the girl who got me this far.

I watch, as others weep when your casket is closed. Longing for what
once was.
They hold their roses.

They are seeing the person they thought they knew, for the last time.

As the crowd simmers down
we are the only one left as you are lowered to your final resting place
with notes and flowers upon flowers.

I gift you a rose | an homage to your given name

Funerals are an opus of drama.
My eyes feel blank and bereaved,

My dear child, I have come to say goodbye.

> *"I fear I am becoming someone you will not like. I fear that*
> *losing you will leave me empty,*
> *staring down the barrel of impending adulthood."*

I take off my glasses- dramatic for the occasion, big, striking, and
black.
Attributes of you that were hidden under shame for far too long.

I cherish the many beautiful parts of you.
I carry them with me so they will not go to waste.

I nurtured you back to health. We became a team. A subconscious
duo.
I showed up for you.

I gave you the kindness, consideration, and love you thought you didn't deserve.

I stopped you from going down the path our abuser chose for us.

I worked so damn hard to take care of you.

I got help.

I let your grievances be heard.

I healed your wounds.

We had to find peace in healing before we could finally grow up.

My child, I release you

Rest now.

May it be long and peaceful.

I gift you the white rose.

"The Peculiar Celebration"

Interlude II

Thank you, Ms.Lauryn Hill.

You taught me how to emote, write, and dream.

This book was written in pursuit of my peace of mind.

"You inspire me, to be the higher me"

I Gotta Find Peace of Mind

by Ms. Lauryn Hill

Home is not a place.

Home is not a singular entity.

Home is a state of being.

Home is stillness.

Home is peace.

Home is comfort.

My first home was the echo of an empty stage.

Home can be the familiarity of your fingertips as they trace piano keys.

Home can be the rustle of the trees.

Home can be the subtle sound of a pen bringing new worlds to life.

Home can be the wind wrapping you in its warm embrace.

Home can be a heartbeat.

At home you are seen

At home you are respected.

At home you are heard

At home you are safe.

I hope your mind is not a place that brings you war.

In the vessel that holds your light, is a house
It's the first one you ever had.

Make it Home.

Our bodies deserve to be decorated and treated with kindness.

It is never too late to reconcile with your body.

And it's never too late to redefine what home means to you.

"Reconstruction"

Darling, you looked at me and my heart fell into disarray.

There is nothing graceful about this poem.
because
There is nothing graceful about me.

When I catch you looking at me
I cannot breathe.
I examine your eyes.

Can you stop looking at me like that?
Like a puzzle you can't crack.
A terrain- you haven't yet explored.

Your eyes shine bright like a kid
In a candy store
Am *I* really that interesting?
I cannot remember because my heart is beating too fast.
It's disorienting.

I notice every inexplicable detail about you and not in the lush grand
romantic way.

The beauty in the small things about you knock me off my feet
until I'm choking on shards of my own dignity.

Because I don't know how to talk to you: so it comes out forced
And then I'm forced to improvise.

Truth is
I always see your eyes
The scrunch of your nose when you make a silly face.
Your hands are small, soft, and delicate in all the ways you are not.
I see you in the soft light of the morning before I have even processed
the enormity of being alive yet.

I see you on that night,
the rise and fall of your chest
falling out of rhythm.

The trepidation in your heart rushed to the shore, revealing itself in
your eyes.

We locked eyes.
And I longed to calm that storm.
I didn't think you had it in you as well.

Anxiety
that wraps around your chest like thorns on the vine.
Sending your whole mind into disarray.

I know, I have more anxiety than most
but it comforted me to see that I took your breath away too.

I thought to myself, we really should kiss.
And before long a small hand found itself at my waist.

Gravity shifts.

We are so close to finding each other's lips.

I inhale

A hand guides me closer until.......

The tension lifts

My mind rests.

"Words I left unsaid"

What if hell was merely the confines of your own ego?

Could you escape it?

-AGENCY

I am *enamored* with you.

My fallen angel,

You send chills down my spine

You are so lovely, and still
heaven sent.

I asked for salvation
and the universe in all her majesty sent me you - to coax the very best out of
me.

I soothed the fury roaring in your soul.
Starving for Revolution; I still went with you.
And with my kisses, cautioned you not to let desire and rage overcome you.

My angel,
you say my name like an oath you intend to keep,
My name naturally slips out your lips *so softly-* it almost sounds like
praying.

Divine, Idyllic, Sacred

One touch and my resolve melts like butter;
my human heart mere putty in your hands.

The melodies you sing are sacred, a hymn I then recite to the heavens.

I hope they are jealous that I get to keep you
and *I* wouldn't dare think of throwing you away.
Instead, I listen to you each day.
I dedicate each day to making you feel seen.

And you, devote your days to making this broken little girl feel hopeful.
I etch my love into you, kisses to intertwine myself with even the most
sensitive parts of you.
You hold my hand as you take what I give.
I wash and mend your broken wings.
You whisper platitudes and sweet nothings into my ear.

We are drunk on the melodic elixir of madness.
Yet, we stay grounded in one another.
Synergy-
Yin and Yang
A gravitational pull so strong -
Even the might of heaven could not take it away.

MY FALLEN ANGEL, I THINK I SHALL MARRY YOU ONE DAY.

As a child, I crafted the worlds I wanted to live in.

I entrenched myself in stories of redemption and reconciliation.

I entertained the innocent flights of fancy that a child dares to dream.

Delusions keep me safe at night,
Assured by nothing but hope that the day will come that my storybook character would be saved.

The day will come when her family will apologize.
The day will come where she will have a mother
a mother
who doesn't need a parent.
The day will come when her family will respect her.
The day will come when the abuse will stop.
The day will come when she will no longer have to play games.

The day *will* come and I *will* get to be a child. | that is the lie I told myself

but it gave me hope to carry, this token of/from the child who dared to dream.

There is no one coming to rewrite this story, beat the "bad guys" and right every wrong.

there is no happy ending that I don't create

And first I must grieve the loss of all the fairytale endings I didn't get.

Release the
"should have been's "

Only I have the power to grant myself deliverance.

-shit

The sanctity of your piece of mind is your first priority.
Not catering to bruised egos

Your heart knows who has earned the right to be granted access
the Others should be denied.

Discernment is Key.

Choose Wisely

-S'il vous plaît, soyez prudent

What are the implications of a society that fails to teach you how to love?

It teaches all the wrong things

It sells you the fantasy.

Infatuation

Obsession

Delusion.

It sells out movies and little girls quake with anticipation of their own duplicitous cinematic love.

No one just tells them the truth.

Explosive chemistry is as beautiful as it is decimating.

that disorienting dissonance is key to understanding the nature of love

Love is a length of rope.

Love is the tool that unites the broken

Love is a weapon.

They laud the heroics and tales of royal grand gestures.
They sold us a mighty good story.

But no one tells you the ways love can be subverted and exploited.

No one tells you that love is a balancing act.

No one tells you that love can trap you inside a hell of your own creation.

No one tells you the ways that love can inflict and inspire violence...
it may be the most dangerous thing of all.

And no one tells you that love, is simply not enough.

Facade

"Be honest with *me,* would you?"

I look into your eyes - hollowed are my eyes and spirit

We have been doing this dance for a while now dear.

This goodbye may kill me.

I'm grown enough to get it done, anyway

Are you?

I see the way you've been holding on to me; desperately

Everything about us is now

                 different.

Sometimes I think you hate me.

But I know that's my inner child speaking.

you couldn't hate me if you tried.
Too much has passed between us

You no longer have any use for me.

I feel it and I

devoted my life force to you.

The worst thing of all is that I
would do it again.

I always had a feeling you-
this life-
would leave me with nothing.

You're pushing me away instead of facing the fact you don't want me
anymore.

And that's okay. I really just need to hear you say it.
I won't
because then you would be getting out too easy.

 I want you to overcome that cowardice
 and look me in my eyes as you let me "free"

I won't pretend empty promises and a gaping hole in my heart
is all I got from this union.
I am the same girl who you fell in love with, just beaten down.

Wiser.

I don't know when the bonds of our union became too heavy for you.
I watched you flounder while you insisted everything was fine-

Like I couldn't see you were fucking drowning.

Everyone said this would happen.

And it has; to be sure
But,
I never
in a million years thought
it would be you, too

Honestly, I haven't been happy in a long time.
The thing that hurts me the most is seeing how misery sits on your face.
Nothing I could have done would remedy the situation.
You did not want me anymore.

Me

I watched that fact settle into your body like bile.

I let it fester.

That light was gone, in your eyes
when you looked at me.

I was no longer special, just the one who you inexplicably- could not
love anymore.

There is a special kind of misery one dances with, when you watch your
own beating heart
fall out of love with you.

So, I sit around and wait for your truth to emerge
in every quiet car ride, in every phone call filled with silence.

I wait

I wait

I Anguish

And I
wait.

Until one day you asked me such a peculiar question.

" Babe...... be honest with *me*..."

Cowardice

There is no currency more valuable than time.

what will you do with the time you are given?

i am finite;
and so are you

so what will you do with the time you are given;
and who will you spend it with?

- AUTONOMY

Delirious

Emotional

Valiant

Obedience

Tiresome

Idealistic

Ownership

Naivety

Deliberate

Emotional

Vulnerable

Open

Thoughtful

Intentional

Opportune

Nourishment

I do not go where I have not been invited.

Why would I?
I have *finally*
stepped into my power as a woman.

Why would I let you take that power away from me?
Why would I put myself
in a space I don't belong?

You are not meant to be in every space

Perhaps you're not ready to be there.

Maybe, you are above them now.

But
Do not stoop to consort with the dust beneath your feet.

You can create *your own* safe spaces.

I find being "palatable"
to be exceptionally overrated.

Who is begging for scraps like a dog,
for a measly invitation?

I Go into places where I am Exalted.

I will not be tolerated or tokenized.

I will not settle. I will not bow. I will not beg.

I will not cower. I will not inquire.

I will not let you make me into a fool.

I do not go where I have not been invited.

"There ain't no motherfucking way."

When I was ripped apart from my abusers I found myself in my friends' loving arms.

I leaned for the very first time
I leaned on my dearest family, with whom I shared not an ounce of blood.
But that didn't fucking matter.
I escaped.

this is usually where the story ends.

No one tells you what happens *after* you nourish your body and slowly nurture yourself back to health.

One day,
you find yourself with a new strength you had absolutely no idea you had.

Nobody tells you how scary it is
to stand up - by yourself.

There is a feeling you cannot shake.

A shift, and you're scared shitless.

It's not that your people aren't there for you.

You're just not in impending and dire crisis anymore

You "did" it.

I survived.

Pills | Twice Daily.

Countless journals | Bursting at the seams.

Intensive Therapy.

All accompanied by the gift of time.

It doesn't take long for me to realize that *I am* finally fucking free

I am not in crisis anymore.

And that is terrifying

I am my own responsibility.

I have to trust that if I fall again, or just stumble

They will be there to catch me

Now,

the people I love facilitate my joy

No longer necessities holding me up,

preventing me from sinking too deep, beyond their reach

       6 feet underneath their own.

"After the credits roll"

a note from the author

Beloved readers, you are my community.

Especially so during this project as I process years of grief, trauma, and strife the only way I know how,
 through art.

I am living my life intentionally for the very first time and documenting the emotional and mental journey.

I extend to you my eternal gratitude for going on this journey with me.

If my art has touched just one of you in a long-lasting, and truly meaningful way, on my last day, I can lay my head to rest knowing I was successful in this life.

You are my legacy. I hope you are better off because this book landed in your hands.

I will end with the immortal words of Nat King Cole.

"I love you for sentimental reasons.

I hope you do believe me"

My dearest reader, *"I have given you my heart."*

Sincerely,

from the bottom of my beating heart
To the very depths of my soul

- Elodie

Song | "I love you for sentimental reasons" by Nat King Cole.

To the women in my life:

Lisa, Lanae, and Katalina*

Thank you.

My special thanks to Katalina for being the best sympathetic ear anyone could have. Your vibrance and warmth has been such a blessing. You encouraged me to keep creating and I am so grateful you did. Your ongoing support has been integral to the completion of this project. Thank you for showing up and most importantly just being yourself.

To everyone I have loved,
Thank you.

To those I cherish,
Thank you.

To my dearest, Elijah

There is nothing on earth that compares to the love we share. As I journey toward abundance and ascension, you have illuminated my path. You are my greatest blessing. It's been a pleasure doing life at your side as your sister. The only reason I am alive making art is because of you. You took care of me until I could finally do it myself. You inspired me to finally care about myself, because I wanted to see myself as you do. I love you.

Thank you.

To Nohemi,
You are a brilliant and patient editor.

Thank you for getting this project off the ground.

You can find Elodie on social media.

INSTAGRAM: @POEMSBYELODIE

TIK-TOK: @ELODIEROSEWRITES

GOODREADS: ELODIE ROSE | POET

STAY TUNED